Organizing Your Home Office for a More Successful You

Organizing Your Home Office for a More Successful You

Diane E. Dunn

THREE SKILLET

ORGANIZING YOUR HOME OFFICE FOR A MORE SUCCESSFUL YOU, Dunn, Diane E.
1st ed.

www.ThreeSkilletPublishing.com

ISBN: 978-1-943189-57-1

A Note from Diane

I started work at a soda fountain in my local mall when I was fifteen. That's when I first became aware of the importance of an organized workspace. From keeping track of the receipts to reloading the ice cream in the displays, if something wasn't where I needed it, it slowed down my service to my customers.

I never forgot that, either, when I moved to a secretarial position in a window replacement shop. I used what I learned at the soda fountain, and I expanded it to improve my customer service to make the clients' experience better. I took phone calls, scheduled home visits, and even helped walk-ins who just showed up without an appointment. It was a lesson I took to heart.

As I moved into telephone sales, became an executive assistant, and even manned the front desk for a large, international organization, one thing became clear to me over and over.

Organization was key to my success no matter where I worked.

When I set up my home office, I started off in a walk-in closet. My skills at organization were crucial to survival in such a small space, but I used what I'd learned over the years, and it worked for me. I was in that closet for years before we moved and I got an entire room that was for my office alone.

Anyone who walks into my home office today will see many of these principles in place. Others I use in my commercial office I share with the Vice President. (Yes, I still work outside the home.) When my schedule begins to swamp me, and I feel pressed for time, do I slip up on these rules occasionally? Everyone does. It only reminds me how important each of these suggestions is for an efficient and productive work space, and I pull out my shredder and my trash can, and I shred it all back into line.

I'm excited to learn how your project goes. Feel free to send before and after pictures to my email inbox at myoffice@dianedunn.org, and I'll post them on my website.

Good luck with designing your perfect home office, and through the process, may you become a more successful you!

Sincerely,
Diane Dunn
www.dianedunn.org

Table of Contents

Walking in Should Be a Joy

Tip No. 1

If you don't have one, install an easy-to-access light switch.

Let all things be done decently and in order.

1 Corinthians 14:40

Tip No. 2

Clear the area around the door for a clutter-free entrance.

Let all things be done decently and in order.

1 Corinthians 14:40

Tip No. 3

Toss out throw rugs to open the space visually.

Let all things be done decently and in order.
1 Corinthians 14:40

Tip No. 4

Choose a decorative tray to drop your keys and other small items.

Let all things be done decently and in order.
1 Corinthians 14:40

Tip No. 5

Place any pet beds in an out-of-the way corner.

Let all things be done decently and in order.

1 Corinthians 14:40

Tip No. 6

Close your eyes for a moment and picture an organized day.

Let all things be done decently and in order.
1 Corinthians 14:40

Tip No. 7

Turn your phone off or to vibrate; your office time is yours.

Let all things be done decently and in order.
1 Corinthians 14:40

Tip No. 8

Keep your favorite scent available to draw you in.

Let all things be done decently and in order.

1 Corinthians 14:40

Tip No. 9

Use several small lamps to focus your visual energy where you intend to spend your day.

Let all things be done decently and in order.

1 Corinthians 14:40

Tip No. 10

Use a sound machine or a small fan to mask outdoor sounds.

Let all things be done decently and in order.
1 Corinthians 14:40

Your Chair Is Your Throne

Tip No. 1

A wheeled chair is ideal for easy movement.

Let all things be done decently and in order.

1 Corinthians 14:40

Tip No. 2

If your office is carpeted, a hard-surface mat will save your legs.

Let all things be done decently and in order.
1 Corinthians 14:40

Tip No. 3

Always use a chair with arms that fit you.

Let all things be done decently and in order.
1 Corinthians 14:40

Tip No. 4

A chair with height adjustment is worth its weight in gold.

Let all things be done decently and in order.

1 Corinthians 14:40

Tip No. 5

Choose a five-roller chair for extra stability.

Let all things be done decently and in order.

1 Corinthians 14:40

Tip No. 6

The darker the chair's upholstery, the better it hides stains.

Let all things be done decently and in order.

1 Corinthians 14:40

Tip No. 7

Never loan your chair; it will take on the shape of whoever sits in it.

Let all things be done decently and in order.
1 Corinthians 14:40

Tip No. 8

A little oil always quiets a squeaky chair (and a complaining spouse).

Let all things be done decently and in order.
1 Corinthians 14:40

Tip No. 9

Adjustable arms allow you to store your chair underneath your desk. It's worth the extra money.

Let all things be done decently and in order.

1 Corinthians 14:40

Tip No. 10

Pay for that built-in headrest. You'll be glad you did.

Let all things be done decently and in order.
1 Corinthians 14:40

Making Your Desk Work for You

Tip No. 1

Never keep out more than one pen.

Let all things be done decently and in order.
1 Corinthians 14:40

Tip No. 2

Clear your desk of distracting mementos.

Let all things be done decently and in order.
1 Corinthians 14:40

Tip No. 3

Use your keyboard tray for your keyboard and your mouse.

Let all things be done decently and in order.
1 Corinthians 14:40

Tip No. 4

Make your mouse wireless; they're inexpensive and worth every penny.

Let all things be done decently and in order.
1 Corinthians 14:40

Tip No. 5

Replace your mousepad regularly.

Let all things be done decently and in order.
1 Corinthians 14:40

Tip No. 6

A footrest under your desk can make a long day into a short one.

Let all things be done decently and in order.
1 Corinthians 14:40

Tip No. 7

Keep a can of wax-free cleaning spray to wipe down your keyboard daily.

Let all things be done decently and in order.

1 Corinthians 14:40

Tip No. 8

Keep all notes on a small bulletin board. When it's full, weed out the old ones.

Let all things be done decently and in order.
1 Corinthians 14:40

Tip No. 9

Keep one desk drawer for essentials and another for paper products.

Let all things be done decently and in order.
1 Corinthians 14:40

Tip No. 10

Use a box under your desk to place things you haven't used in two months, then toss them each Friday.

Let all things be done decently and in order.

1 Corinthians 14:40

Keeping Your Shelves on Par With Your Desk

Tip No. 1

Put reference books on a bottom shelf.

Let all things be done decently and in order.

1 Corinthians 14:40

Tip No. 2

One picture is all you need;
move the rest into the den.

Let all things be done decently and in order.
1 Corinthians 14:40

Tip No. 3

Organize your books by topic on each shelf.

Let all things be done decently and in order.

1 Corinthians 14:40

Tip No. 4

Never place anything on your shelves "just for now."

Let all things be done decently and in order.
1 Corinthians 14:40

Tip No. 5

Dust on a regular basis. (Use the wax-free spray from your desk!)

Let all things be done decently and in order.
1 Corinthians 14:40

Tip No. 6

Keep out one small stack of envelopes. (We'll deal with the rest later.)

Let all things be done decently and in order.

1 Corinthians 14:40

Tip No. 7

Extra pens and pencils need to fit in one container.

Let all things be done decently and in order.
1 Corinthians 14:40

Tip No. 8

Enclosed, decorative boxes on the top of the shelf are great for seldom-used items.

Let all things be done decently and in order.
1 Corinthians 14:40

Tip No. 9

Save half of one shelf for borrowed books or supplies you will use only for a short time.

Let all things be done decently and in order.
1 Corinthians 14:40

Tip No. 10

Never let anything from your desk bleed over onto your shelf.

Let all things be done decently and in order.
1 Corinthians 14:40

Your Filing Cabinet Is Key

Tip No. 1

Four drawers are a must, even if you give up room for something else.

Let all things be done decently and in order.
1 Corinthians 14:40

Tip No. 2

A lock is vital on your filing cabinet, even in your own home.

Let all things be done decently and in order.
1 Corinthians 14:40

Tip No. 3

Black, black, black. A black filing cabinet goes with anything.

Let all things be done decently and in order.
1 Corinthians 14:40

Tip No. 4

Use stickies to temporarily label your drawers while you organize them.

Let all things be done decently and in order.
1 Corinthians 14:40

Tip No. 5

The top drawer is your personal drawer, for only you.

Let all things be done decently and in order.
1 Corinthians 14:40

Tip No. 6

The second drawer is your business drawer, the one you access most often.

Let all things be done decently and in order.
1 Corinthians 14:40

Tip No. 7

The third drawer is for extras, like envelopes (See, we got to it.) or extra printer paper.

Let all things be done decently and in order.
1 Corinthians 14:40

Tip No. 8

The bottom drawer is perfect for seldom used files such as old tax forms.

Let all things be done decently and in order.

1 Corinthians 14:40

Tip No. 9

Keep a snack in your filing cabinet to save run time to the kitchen.

Let all things be done decently and in order.

1 Corinthians 14:40

Tip No. 10

Always lock your files every night.

Let all things be done decently and in order.
1 Corinthians 14:40

Decorations for a More Successful Day

Tip No. 1

A simple decorating scheme eliminates distractions.

Let all things be done decently and in order.
1 Corinthians 14:40

Tip No. 2

A lamp with a plain shade gives better light.

Let all things be done decently and in order.
1 Corinthians 14:40

Tip No. 3

Paint your walls a neutral
and pleasant color.

Let all things be done decently and in order.
1 Corinthians 14:40

Tip No. 4

Choose wall art that doesn't compete for your attention.

Let all things be done decently and in order.
1 *Corinthians* 14:40

Tip No. 5

One large picture is better than numerous small ones.

Let all things be done decently and in order.
1 Corinthians 14:40

Tip No. 6

Use matte photo frames to cut down on reflected light.

Let all things be done decently and in order.
1 Corinthians 14:40

Tip No. 7

Choose one inspiration piece to display in a prominent place.

Let all things be done decently and in order.
1 Corinthians 14:40

Tip No. 8

Add an "L" to your desk, even if it's a portable table or a low shelf.

Let all things be done decently and in order.
1 Corinthians 14:40

Tip No. 9

A simple wall clock will help you keep track of time.

Let all things be done decently and in order.
1 Corinthians 14:40

Tip No. 10

A desktop fan is great for those days filled with stressful deadlines.

Let all things be done decently and in order.
1 Corinthians 14:40

Making the Area Under Your Desk Work for You

Tip No. 1

Choose a trash can that fits under your desk.

Let all things be done decently and in order.
1 Corinthians 14:40

Tip No. 2

Empty your trash can every day.

Let all things be done decently and in order.
1 Corinthians 14:40

Tip No. 3

Stack enclosed boxes under your "L" labeled with clients' names.

Let all things be done decently and in order.

1 Corinthians 14:40

Tip No. 4

Organize your clients' boxes by color.

Let all things be done decently and in order.

1 Corinthians 14:40

Tip No. 5

Stack your clients' boxes in the order of your upcoming deadlines.

Let all things be done decently and in order.
1 Corinthians 14:40

Tip No. 6

A small shelf under your "L" is perfect for extra supplies.

Let all things be done decently and in order.

1 Corinthians 14:40

Tip No. 7

Keep two rulers on your shelf, one short and the second extra long.

Let all things be done decently and in order.
1 Corinthians 14:40

Tip No. 8

Small bins of gum or mints will help you get through the day.

Let all things be done decently and in order.
1 Corinthians 14:40

Tip No. 9

Select one shelf or box to be your "just for now" spot.

Let all things be done decently and in order.

1 Corinthians 14:40

Tip No. 10

Use one shelf or box for a "junk" box for things you might want to throw away.

Let all things be done decently and in order.
1 Corinthians 14:40

Extra Workspace

Tip No. 1

A fold-down desk or portable table makes for instant workspace.

Let all things be done decently and in order.
1 Corinthians 14:40

Tip No. 2

Your portable workspace must be just that: portable. Nothing permanent goes there.

Let all things be done decently and in order.
1 Corinthians 14:40

Tip No. 3

Store your fold-down portable workspace behind a door for a clean look when the door is open.

Let all things be done decently and in order.
1 Corinthians 14:40

Tip No. 4

Your portable table can extend your office into a hallway or adjacent room in emergencies.

Let all things be done decently and in order.
1 Corinthians 14:40

Tip No. 5

Don't forget your keyboard tray. Put a shallow container behind your keyboard for notepads or markers.

Let all things be done decently and in order.
1 Corinthians 14:40

Tip No. 6

An open drawer makes a perfect desk extension. Lay a clipboard over it for a work surface.

Let all things be done decently and in order.
1 Corinthians 14:40

Tip No. 7

Claim a spare dresser for an office credenza.

Let all things be done decently and in order.
1 Corinthians 14:40

Tip No. 8

Replace drawers in the dresser with baskets laid on their side for easy access.

Let all things be done decently and in order.
1 Corinthians 14:40

Tip No. 9

Drill a hole in the top of the dresser to organize lamp and printer cords.

Let all things be done decently and in order.
1 Corinthians 14:40

Tip No. 10

A windowsill makes a great bookcase.

Let all things be done decently and in order.
1 Corinthians 14:40

Making Your Office Your Own

Tip No. 1

Hang a sign on the door you can flip from "Come In" to "Busy."

Let all things be done decently and in order.
1 Corinthians 14:40

Tip No. 2

Hang a small marker board on your door for your family to leave messages in your "Busy" time.

Let all things be done decently and in order.
1 Corinthians 14:40

Tip No. 3

Spread several brightly decorated tissue boxes around the room.

Let all things be done decently and in order.

1 Corinthians 14:40

Tip No. 4

An extra chair next to a lamp is great for reading your reports.

Let all things be done decently and in order.

1 Corinthians 14:40

Tip No. 5

Find room for a loveseat or sofa to sneak short naps.

Let all things be done decently and in order.

1 Corinthians 14:40

Tip No. 6

A simple coat hook for visitors will remind them not to forget their things. (It works for purses, too!)

Let all things be done decently and in order.

1 Corinthians 14:40

Tip No. 7

A favorite pillow will help your back when you've worked a long day.

Let all things be done decently and in order.

1 Corinthians 14:40

Tip No. 8

Stash a small refrigerator under your desk "L" or use it as a small table by your chair.

Let all things be done decently and in order.
1 Corinthians 14:40

Tip No. 9

A plug-in air freshener filled with your favorite scent takes up almost no room.

Let all things be done decently and in order.

1 Corinthians 14:40

Tip No. 10

Your screen saver on your computer is perfect for your family photos.

Let all things be done decently and in order.
1 Corinthians 14:40

Making a Closet Do Extra Duty

Tip No. 1

Your office closet is now yours. Empty out everything else.

Let all things be done decently and in order.
1 Corinthians 14:40

Tip No. 2

Shorten the clothing rod to no more than two feet.

Let all things be done decently and in order.

1 Corinthians 14:40

Tip No. 3

Stackable file boxes keep rarely used items out of sight.

Let all things be done decently and in order.

1 Corinthians 14:40

Tip No. 4

Always label each box with a lined sheet of adhesive-backed paper. Adjust the list as you move things in or out.

Let all things be done decently and in order.

1 Corinthians 14:40

Tip No. 5

Keep the floor clear. You can't use what you can't get to.

Let all things be done decently and in order.

1 Corinthians 14:40

Tip No. 6

A foldable stepstool gives you access to things high up.

Let all things be done decently and in order.
1 Corinthians 14:40

Tip No. 7

Use that empty space. Install a sturdy shelf around the ceiling for reams of paper or odd-size boxes of supplies.

Let all things be done decently and in order.
1 Corinthians 14:40

Tip No. 8

Store your portable paper trimmer at waist level for easy access.

Let all things be done decently and in order.
1 Corinthians 14:40

Tip No. 9

A pegboard on the back wall is great for scissors or other hard to store items.

Let all things be done decently and in order.
1 Corinthians 14:40

Tip No. 10

Label each peg so things always go back where they belong.

Let all things be done decently and in order.
1 Corinthians 14:40

Organizing Your Computer to Maximize Your Day

Tip No. 1

Zip tie your cables behind your monitor for an uncluttered look.

Let all things be done decently and in order.
1 Corinthians 14:40

Tip No. 2

Cut a hole in the back of a decorative, covered box for power bricks and unsightly cords.

Let all things be done decently and in order.

1 Corinthians 14:40

Tip No. 3

A second monitor doubles your efficiency . . . the larger the better.

Let all things be done decently and in order.
1 Corinthians 14:40

Tip No. 4

Create desktop folders on your screen to store seldom-used icons.

Let all things be done decently and in order.
1 Corinthians 14:40

Tip No. 5

Purchase several USB extenders to avoid having to search the back of your computer to plug in temporary devices.

Let all things be done decently and in order.
1 Corinthians 14:40

Tip No. 6

Have a small lamp that shines on your keyboard.

Let all things be done decently and in order.
1 Corinthians 14:40

Tip No. 7

Keep your keyboard at elbow level. Adjust your chair up or down if necessary.

Let all things be done decently and in order.
1 Corinthians 14:40

Tip No. 8

If someone else must use your computer, give them a separate user account and login password.

Let all things be done decently and in order.

1 Corinthians 14:40

Tip No. 9

Tap the control key to wake your computer from its sleep cycle.

Let all things be done decently and in order.

1 Corinthians 14:40

Tip No. 10

Lock your computer at the end of every day, even if no one else is home.

Let all things be done decently and in order.
1 Corinthians 14:40

The Purpose in Plants

Tip No. 1

Green is restful to the eyes.

Let all things be done decently and in order.
1 Corinthians 14:40

Tip No. 2

Keep several small plants you don't mind gifting to special visitors.

Let all things be done decently and in order.
1 Corinthians 14:40

Tip No. 3

Plants can be moved to hide inconvenient cords or staplers.

Let all things be done decently and in order.
1 Corinthians 14:40

Tip No. 4

Plants listen and never repeat your frustrations.

Let all things be done decently and in order.
1 Corinthians 14:40

Tip No. 5

Plants are oxygen generators. You need oxygen.

Let all things be done decently and in order.
1 Corinthians 14:40

Tip No. 6

Your office will smell fresher
with plants.

Let all things be done decently and in order.
1 Corinthians 14:40

Tip No. 7

Healthy plants tell your visitors you are conscientious in your work.

Let all things be done decently and in order.
1 Corinthians 14:40

Tip No. 8

Plants in bloom add bursts of color and brighten the ambience of your workspace.

Let all things be done decently and in order.
1 Corinthians 14:40

Tip No. 9

If a plant is droopy, it's time to take a break from your work. Water your plant.

Let all things be done decently and in order.
1 Corinthians 14:40

Tip No. 10

If all your plants die, it's time to refocus how dedicated you are to your work.

Let all things be done decently and in order.
1 Corinthians 14:40

Television Pros and Cons

Tip No. 1

A high-definition television makes a great second computer monitor.

Let all things be done decently and in order.
1 Corinthians 14:40

Tip No. 2

Balance your day to keep your "office" time distinct from your "TV" time.

Let all things be done decently and in order.

1 Corinthians 14:40

Tip No. 3

Can you justify television time during office hours? If not, turn it off.

Let all things be done decently and in order.
1 Corinthians 14:40

Tip No. 4

Your office television isn't a second TV for family members when your "Busy" sign is up. (Or any other time you are working!)

Let all things be done decently and in order.

1 Corinthians 14:40

Tip No. 5

Use the weekend to plan a special "movie" date in your office with one family member. You'll make them feel special. (And they'll respect your office "Busy" time more!)

Let all things be done decently and in order.

1 Corinthians 14:40

Tip No. 6

Keep the remotes in one place so they never get lost.

Let all things be done decently and in order.
1 Corinthians 14:40

Tip No. 7

Make your office TV off limits after bedtime. (And remember, your office door is locked at night!)

Let all things be done decently and in order.
1 Corinthians 14:40

Tip No. 8

Set your favorite channels so you don't waste time scrolling through useless ones.

Let all things be done decently and in order.

1 Corinthians 14:40

Tip No. 9

If your TV breaks, don't throw it out. The flat, glossy screen makes a great sticky note display.

Let all things be done decently and in order.
1 Corinthians 14:40

Tip No. 10

If you can live without it, not having a TV in your office is your best production stimulator of all.

Let all things be done decently and in order.
1 Corinthians 14:40

A Window Without a View

Tip No. 1

No view? Install blinds on all windows.

Let all things be done decently and in order.
1 Corinthians 14:40

Tip No. 2

Got a view? Keep the blinds closed while you're working to eliminate distractions.

Let all things be done decently and in order.
1 Corinthians 14:40

Tip No. 3

Blackout curtains help maintain a consistent room temperature.

Let all things be done decently and in order.

1 Corinthians 14:40

Tip No. 4

Blackout curtains also keep your neighbors from knowing when you work far into the night.

Let all things be done decently and in order.

1 Corinthians 14:40

Tip No. 5

Install an inexpensive awning or a tree just outside a sunny window.

Let all things be done decently and in order.
1 Corinthians 14:40

Tip No. 6

Install two screws in the jam to allow fresh air in but not intruders.

Let all things be done decently and in order.
1 Corinthians 14:40

Tip No. 7

Patterned contact paper on the glass gives you light without distractions.

Let all things be done decently and in order.
1 Corinthians 14:40

Tip No. 8

Hanging a stained-glass window or a patterned pull-down shade is another option.

Let all things be done decently and in order.
1 Corinthians 14:40

Tip No. 9

Keep any light from a window that can't be obscured at your back.

Let all things be done decently and in order.
1 Corinthians 14:40

Tip No. 10

Start and end your day at your window reminding yourself that there's a world outside your office, and it belongs to you, too. Get outside and experience it!

Let all things be done decently and in order.

1 Corinthians 14:40

Getting Your Printing in Line

Tip No. 1

A wireless printing station
can be placed anywhere.

Let all things be done decently and in order.
1 Corinthians 14:40

Tip No. 2

If you must have cords, keep them corralled with zip ties.

Let all things be done decently and in order.

1 Corinthians 14:40

Tip No. 3

Never place anything on top of your printers.

Let all things be done decently and in order.
1 Corinthians 14:40

Tip No. 4

Fill the paper tray. (But remember where you've stored the rest!)

Let all things be done decently and in order.

1 Corinthians 14:40

Tip No. 5

Ink keeps better in a dry, cool location (in your closet or in your dresser-credenza).

Let all things be done decently and in order.
1 Corinthians 14:40

Tip No. 6

Dust your printer weekly.

Let all things be done decently and in order.
1 Corinthians 14:40

Tip No. 7

Run the printer's cleaning cycle. (This really helps!)

Let all things be done decently and in order.
1 Corinthians 14:40

Tip No. 8

Organize small quantities of specialty papers in file folders in your file cabinet.

Let all things be done decently and in order.
1 Corinthians 14:40

Tip No. 9

Shred old print jobs you won't be using.

Let all things be done decently and in order.
1 Corinthians 14:40

Tip No. 10

Get a good shredder. It's a must for every home office. (This could have been first on my list!)

Let all things be done decently and in order.
1 Corinthians 14:40

— Space for Notes —

Let all things be done decently and in order.

1 Corinthians 14:40

— Space for Notes —

Let all things be done decently and in order.

1 Corinthians 14:40

— Space for Notes —

Let all things be done decently and in order.

1 Corinthians 14:40

— Space for Notes —

Good luck with your new office space. Share these tips with your friends. Everyone deserves a refreshing place in which to work. You deserve to enjoy yours!

Wishing you the best,
Diane

www.ingramcontent.com/pod-product-compliance
Lightning Source LLC
Chambersburg PA
CBHW060923040426
42445CB00011B/770
9781943189571